P9-CND-138

God's Tender Mercy

REFLECTIONS ON FORGIVENESS

JOAN CHITTISTER

God's tender mercy

Reflections on FORGIVENESS

For more information about Joan Chittister, OSB, please visit her Web site: www.benetvision.org

Second printing 2011

TWENTY-THIRD PUBLICATIONS
A Division of Bayard
One Montauk Avenue, Suite 200
New London, CT 06320
(860) 437-3012 or (800) 321-0411
www.23rdpublications.com

ISBN 978-1-58595-799-6
Library of Congress Catalog Card Number: 2010925840

Printed in the U.S.A.

CONTENTS

Jesus

On Sin and Forgiveness

We do a great number of things "religiously," as if they were sacred, with the intensity of the saints, in other words. We do our accounting religiously, we visit our mothers religiously, we go to the kids' soccer games religiously, we walk the dog religiously, we count sins religiously, and we practice our religion religiously—meaning that we do the things we're supposed to do and we do them all the time. And we do them very well. And we do them more often than anyone else. We do them so well, in fact, that we have come to think that the very act of doing them is what makes us holy.

To be righteous, on the other hand, is to do what is godly, to be decent, to commit ourselves to what is above and beyond the trappings of religion, to strive for the essence of religion, which, if we are to believe what Jesus teaches, is clearly the open-handed, foolish, measureless, boundless embrace of the unembraceable.

The most religious thing of all Jesus shows us may be the loving acceptance of those who have trouble doing what is "religious" and "right," however socially correct, however upstanding it may be, however correct they themselves would like to be.

That's where we begin to get a little nervous. That's where the spluttering starts: With that kind of loose-living attitude, what would happen to moral standards? What would happen to the moral fiber of the nation? What would happen to the neighborhood? What would happen to the family, the church, the town, the office, the school if we tolerated deviance, if we didn't stop such deviations, if we didn't require good, upstanding, moral behavior? In fact, that's the trouble these days, isn't it? That's the "L" word. We've been "liberal." We've become lax. We've deteriorated. Or rather, they have deteriorated. We have not. And so the new religion, which is really only more of the old one dressed up in indignation and sour shouts of doom, is setting in. The punitive, the authoritarian, the conservative—meaning reactionary—is becoming commonplace. We want longer prison sentences for first-time offenders. We want "three strikes and you're out," a "throw-away-the-key" approach to small-time repeaters whose harm has been only to themselves. We're not interested in protecting the innocent; we want to kill the killers. We want the dissenters silenced. We want the nonconformists excommunicated. We want the rebels reduced to nothing. We want law and order.

So intent are we on religion that we have forgotten righteousness. We can't understand the Helen Prejeans who walk to our electric chairs with the condemned. We have no time for crafty lawyers who plea-bargain for the people our newspapers convict. We deplore judges who give reasonable sentences to decent people who have found themselves in indecent situations. We wonder about those who consort with the people we suspect. We look with a touch of bewilderment at all those people who treat lovingly the ones we cannot yet love because we ourselves are still more religious than righteous. So much for Jesus with thieves. So much for Jesus with tax collectors. So much for Jesus with women taken in adultery. So much, indeed, for a gospel riddled with the unacceptable, the suspect, the devious and the weak—for the lepers and the Samaritans and the women.

It isn't, of course, that there's no place for accountability. It's just that there's no place for condemnation once we face our own sins. The problem is simply that there's no place for stoning if we are the ones supposed to be pure enough to do it.

In the story of the woman taken in adultery, Jesus is confronted with a sinner about whose punishment the law was plain. The Pharisee's question of what to do with her was an easy one. Jesus, if religious, should have condemned her. But Jesus, the righteous one, did not.

What is really going on here? What's lenten—repentant—about that? To understand what this gospel is calling us to do, we must think of more than law and sin here. We must at the same time think of Sadducees and Pharisees and Jesus.

The Sadducees were the archconservatives, the clerical caste, the ultra orthodox of Judaism. They found the fullness of religion in the law and their role in preserving it. The Pharisees were the liberals of the establishment. They loved the law enough to allow it to develop and to diffuse it throughout the whole community of Israel.

The problem is that Jesus was neither a Sadducee nor a Pharisee, neither a conservative nor a liberal. The fact is that Jesus was too liberal even for the liberals. Jesus didn't let the law become a barrier between him and the person in front of him. Jesus was a radical. Jesus was a lover. Jesus was a radical lover.

And in this story, Jesus' message is plain: Beware of letting sin consume you. No, not yours. Theirs. The fact is—have we forgotten as did the Pharisees in the gospel?—that we have more than enough of our own sin to struggle through.

Surely we are being told much more in this gospel than the fact that we, too, have sinned, something we know only too well in the depths of our dark hearts. Maybe we are really being told that if the world is really deteriorating, it may not be them who are doing it after all. Maybe what is really disintegrating now is the amount of love and listening it takes if the world is to be propelled back into a holy, healthy, happy existence that no amount of force and fear can achieve.

More important still, perhaps the message is more necessary than ever in this world intent on heavy sentences and excommunications and social shunnings. If you yourself are without sin, go ahead.

There are people aplenty out there, struggling, trying, hurting, failing. Feel free: Hunt them down. Grind them under. Count them out. Throw them away. Chortle over their shame. Go ahead. Throw the first stone.

Now that would really be a sin.

CHAPTER 1

Divine Mercy

The Audacity of Mercy

Thomas Ann Hines, a divorced mother of an only child, learned mercy the hard way. When her son, a freshman at college, lay murdered by a seventeen-year-old drifter who first solicited a ride from him and then, when he got in the car, turned a gun on the young driver, Thomas Ann descended into a pit of anger and vengeance. The murder was a random, groundless, indefensible act. And her son was not the only person who died that night—Thomas Ann was alone, distraught, full of the kind of pain and hate that paralyzes the heart and stops life in its tracks, even for the living.

Her son, a good boy, a successful student, the hope of her life was gone. She herself was completely alone now, without a future, without hope, without any reason, it seemed, to live.

But thirteen years later, Thomas Ann Hines visited her son's killer in prison, intent only on getting information about the night of the killing. But when, in the course of the conversation the young man put his face down on the small table at which they sat and began to sob, she touched the man. And she got to know him.

The story shocked the country. "How could she do such a thing?" people asked. Or, more to the point, perhaps, they asked themselves the question, "Could I ever do such a thing? Could I possibly show mercy to someone who had done something so senseless, so heinous, so destructive to me?"

Thomas Ann's answer to the question was a simple one: "If my son was sitting in this room," she said, "I'd want someone to reach out a hand and lift him up."

The story is not only a moving one, it is an enlightening one for all of us. It teaches us something very important about mercy.

Mercy is what God does for us. Mercy discounts the economic sense of love and faith and care for a person and lives out of a divine sense of love instead. Mercy gives a human being who does not "deserve" love, love. And why? Because, the Scriptures answer, God knows of what we are made.

The fact is that we are all made of the same thing: clay, the dust of the earth, the frail, fragile, shapeless thing from which we come and to which we will all return someday. We are all capable of the same things. Our only hope is that when we are all sitting somewhere bereft, exposed, outcast, humiliated and rejected by the rest of society, someone, somewhere will "reach out a hand and lift us up."

❧ Every one of us is capable of every sinful thing. Most of us have simply never had the opportunity or the anger or the sense of desolation it takes to do it. While we're being grateful for that, it behooves us to be merciful to those who have.

❧ Mercy is my answer to my own weaknesses. When those weaknesses erupt in me, may those around me remember their own. "If you wish to receive mercy," St. John Chrysostom wrote, "show mercy to your neighbor."

❧ The mercy and understanding I show to others is the degree of mercy, the kind of understanding I will get when I need it most. To be without mercy is to be yet without an honest awareness of our own humanity.

❧ It is one thing to be righteous; it is another thing to be merciful. Righteousness only confirms us in our pride. Mercy is a sign of humility.

❧ Mercy is what enables us to raise law above the stringency of legalism to the ultimate level of human idealism. "Mercy," Thomas Aquinas wrote, "is the fulfillment of justice, not its abolition."

❦ When we understand why people do things, we have the capacity to change life for the better at its very roots.

❦ To thirst for the punishment of another is to abandon ourselves to the kind of standards we know down deep we cannot keep.

❦ We pray for mercy; we expect mercy. What we find difficult to do is to be merciful to those in need of it. Or as George Eliot says, "We hand folks over to God's mercy, and show none ourselves."

❦ The great spiritual question is not whether or not this person, this situation deserves mercy. It is about whether or not we ourselves are capable of showing it.

❦ The major holy-making moment in our own lives may be when we receive the mercy we know we do not deserve. Then, we may never again substitute disdain for understanding, rejection for openness, legalism for justice. "I think perhaps it is a better world," Helen Waddell writes, "if one has a broken heart. Then one is quick to recognize it, elsewhere."

🌸 Learning to withhold judgment is difficult in a media-driven world but essential in a better one. "Forgiveness," Christian Baldwin writes, "is the act of admitting we are like other people."

🌸 Mercy is learned first in the human heart. "If you haven't forgiven yourself something," Dolores Huerta writes, "how can you forgive others?"

🌸 Not uncommonly, those who are self-righteous are most sinful themselves. Because they hate themselves for what they are, they can't possibly be merciful to anyone else.

🌸 Because history shows us that the church is a sinful church, it is the very place in which we should be able to find the greatest degree of mercy, of understanding, of compassion, of non-judgmentalism.

🌺 To be merciful is to be kind, to be open, to be trusting, to be a friend. Mercy, Shakespeare writes, "is twice blest. It blesseth him that gives and him that takes." It is when we show mercy that we may be closest to God.

🌺 Mercy is what makes us, keeps us, available to one another. It opens our heart to strangers. It enables hospitality. It is the glue of the human race. Tennessee Williams understood the relationship of mercy to human interdependence when he wrote, "I have always depended on the kindness of strangers."

🌺 Coming to understand that there is nothing unforgivable in life is the beginning of real love.

🌺 Mercy is the trait of those who realize their own weakness enough to be kind to those who are struggling with theirs. It is, as well, the measure of the God-life in us. "The weak," Gandhi wrote, "can never forgive. Forgiveness is the attribute of the strong."

🌸 Beware those who show no mercy. They are dangerous people because they have either not faced themselves or are lying to themselves about what they find there.

🌸 "We are all sinners," we say, and then smile the words away. But the essayist Montaigne was clear about it: "There is no one so good," he wrote, "who, were they to submit all their thoughts and actions to the laws, would not deserve hanging ten times in life."

🌸 It is our very weaknesses that enable us to understand the power, the necessity of mercy.

The Sufi mystic Mishkat al-Masabaih reminds us, when we are overwhelmed by our own inadequacies, our own diversions from the straight paths of life, that the mercy of God is always greater than the sin of being too humanly human. He writes: "She who approaches near to Me one span, I will approach near to her one cubit; and she who approaches near to Me one cubit, I will approach near to her one fathom; and whoever approaches Me walking, I will come to her running; and she who meets Me with sins equivalent to the whole world, I will greet her with forgiveness equal to it."

The mercy we show to others is what assures us that we do not need to worry about being perfect ourselves. All we really need to do is to make the effort to be the best we can be, knowing we will often fail. Then, the mercy of others, the mercy of God is certain for us, as well. "The only thing we can offer to God of value," St. Catherine of Sienna said, "is to give our love to people as unworthy of it as we are of God's love."

To hold others to standards higher than our standards for ourselves is to live in constant agitation, personal, national, and global. "Unless it extends the circle of its compassion to all living things," Michael Nagler writes, "humanity will not itself find peace."

🌿 To become "God-like" is the most common—and the most elusive—of all spiritual aspirations. What can that injunction—that desire—possibly mean? A medieval mystic answers the question directly. "When are we like God?" the mystic Mechthild of Magdeburg writes. "I will tell you. Insofar as we love compassion and practice it steadfastly, to that extent, do we resemble the heavenly Creator who practices these things ceaselessly in us."

🌿 When we, too, "know of what we're made," there is no room in us for anything but mercy for the other. "Being all fashioned of the self-same dust," Longfellow wrote, "let us be merciful as well as just."

🌿 Mercy takes us outside ourselves. It makes us one with the rest of the world. Or as Martin Luther King, Jr. reminds us, "The first question which the priest and the Levite asked was, 'If I stop to help this man, what will happen to me?' But the Good Samaritan reversed the question. He said: 'If I don't stop to help this man, what will happen to him?'"

🌿 A sign in Springdale, Connecticut, makes the whole subject clear. It reads: "There is so much good in the worst of us and so much bad in the best of us, that it's rather hard to tell which of us ought to reform the rest of us."

🌿 Strange, isn't it? We expect that God will show us mercy; but, too often, we show so little ourselves. We believe fiercely in capital punishment; we tolerate the thought of nuclear war; we suspect whatever is unlike ourselves. If heaven is based on the same punitive, violent, and segregating principles, we are all in trouble.

The strangest of all human phenomena, perhaps, is that we take God's mercy for granted for ourselves but find it so hard to be merciful ourselves. If there were any proof needed that God is completely "Other," this is surely it.

Perhaps forgiveness is the last thing mentioned in the Creed because it is the last thing learned in life. Perhaps none of us can understand the forgiveness of God until we ourselves have learned to forgive. Perhaps we cannot understand the goodness of God to us because we are so seldom that good to others.

On the contrary, we want mercy for ourselves but exact justice for the remainder of humankind. God, on the other hand, the Creed implies, desires justice but gives mercy like a rushing river, gushes mercy like a running stream. (Joan Chittister, *In Search of Belief*)

"It is often the most wicked who know the nearest path to the shrine," the Japanese proverb reminds us. Don't let anybody fool you: Goodness is as goodness does. Be careful who you call bad simply because the "good" people have named them so. God, it seems, is far less quick to judge.

CHAPTER 2

Forgive Us Our Sins

Forgive Yourself

I long ago learned that sin is not always what meets the eye. I remember the lesson well.

My father had been out of work—on strike—for weeks. It was shortly after the war and the unions were pressing for higher wages and better benefits after a long period of hard work and personal sacrifice. I was very small but very aware that no work meant no money. I was worried about us as a family.

How would we live if my father had no job? And my mother was worried about my worrying. So one night, after another day of union violence, my father scooped me up out of my bed and carried me, blanket trailing, to the windows overlooking the main street of the little steel town where we lived. Then he made me tell him what I saw across the street. "A grocery store," I said. And what did I see in the front of the store, he wanted to know. "Windows," I said. "Right, Jo," my dad said, "and as long as there are windows on grocery stores, you and your mother will eat." I was horrified. "Daddy," I said, "you wouldn't break that window and steal things, would you?" After all, what would Sister say at school if she ever heard anyone say such a thing? I felt his arms tighten around me. "Honey," my father said, "when people have nothing to eat, it is not a sin for them to steal food."

In another story I recall from my childhood, the people down the street got divorced after years of quarreling and night after night of violence. In an age when divorce was unheard of anywhere, I was horrified then, too. Wasn't divorce a sin? I asked.

"Joan," my mother said, "it's far more sinful for those people to go on destroying one another and their children than it is for them to admit that they need to start over again for all their sakes."

Sin, I learned clearly, had more to do with how it affects our humanity and the lives of other people than it does with simply breaking the rules. It was a life lesson of awesome proportions. Being perfect is not always perfect at all. And sometimes keeping the rules, I came to understand, can be more sinful than breaking them.

"If you want to be properly sinful," the wag wrote, "it is not necessary to break the law. Just keep it to perfection." It is people who refuse compassion on the grounds of law that break the heart of God.

We spend a lot of time worrying about "sins of commission"—about things we've done in life, and almost none worrying about "sins of omission"— about the things we've to do. And so, as a result, we have neglected children, social agencies that go begging for volunteers, justice issues ignored because it's not my problem. But strangely enough, I am the only solution.

🌾 We remember the times we scolded the children too harshly but we forget when we took their goodness for granted and neglected to hug them. We worry about the lies we've told as we've gone through life but we worry not a bit about the times we stood silent in the face of disapproval and failed to say a saving truth. We think about stealing but we don't think that failing to give when we could give is also a sin. Sin is as much an attitude of mind as it is a body of behaviors.

🌾 Sin and evil are not the same things. Sin has something to do with failing to be the best of what we are trying to be. Evil is malice unleashed against another with intent to do them harm. Sin is in the air we breathe. It goes with growing. Evil has the smell of sulphur to it.

🔖 The major moral question has got to be why Jesus showed special love to sinners. Surely the answer must be that each of them had the virtue to admit their need for mercy. Most of the rest of us insist on defending our actions and arguing our essential correctness.

🔖 Be at least as afraid of the kind of virtue that gives us the right to condemn everyone else as you are of a few private sins. Arrogance commits us to a community of one. There is nothing to be gained there.

🔖 Don't confuse weakness with sin. Most of us struggle with something we never quite conquer. It is precisely that struggle that can become the stuff of compassion with others.

🔖 Sin changes with age. In youth it is born out of impulse; in later years it is based in calculation. The first stage requires the ability to discriminate and the development of control. It's a period of experimentation that can end in wisdom. But at a later stage, when we have really come to "know good from evil," sin requires that we review the entire value system that drives us. Something has gone seriously awry. And in the end it is not just what our sin does to other people that counts; it is what sin does to us that matters deeply, as well.

❧ When people steal and lie and wallow in excesses, bask in sloth and feed their lusts, we call it sin. When corporations do it we call it good business and success, the art of the deal, and Third World wage scales. Interesting, isn't it?

❧ There are some things that can be learned only by sin. The history of sainthood is a history of sin: Teresa of Avila, Ignatius of Loyola, Charles de Foucauld all struggled their way to God as we do. Only when, like them, we discover the depths of our own neediness can we begin to discover our strengths and God's mercy.

❧ People who have never faced their own sins are people who have yet to know themselves. But without self-knowledge, real spiritual development is impossible. Then, though we may be religious, we have yet to be spiritual.

❧ Annie Dillard tells a story about a tribesman who said to the missionary, "If I did not know about God and sin, would I go to hell?" And the priest said, "Oh, no, if you didn't know about God and sin, God would not send you to hell." "Then why," the tribesman said, "did you tell me?"

❧ The important thing to remember is, as Igor Stravinsky says, that "sin cannot be undone, only forgiven." What we do to ourselves or others stays in the soul like dust in the air. We cannot undo it. We can only begin again. For that reason, God has no memory.

❧ Those who must be perfect simply cannot afford to fail. For them, perfection rests in perfection, not in learning how to recover from the struggles that make a human human. A society that is based on perfectionism, then, never says it's sorry, never does penance, and never really repents. The perfect simply cling to their perfectionism. It is a sickly condition of the soul.

✣ "Who is closer to God," the seeker asked, "the saint or the sinner?" "Why, the sinner, of course," the elder said. "But how can that be?" the seeker asked. "Because," the elder said, "every time a person sins they break the cord that binds them to God. But every time God forgives them, the cord is knotted again. And so, thanks to the mercy of God, the cord gets shorter and the sinner closer to God." It's true, isn't it? We learn from sin the goodness of God— and then our shame is exceeded only by our love.

✣ "God doesn't punish sin," the mystic Julian of Norwich teaches. "Sin punishes sin." It makes sense. If greed is our sin, we shall be forever intent on having more. If anger is our sin, we will be consumed by emotional imbalance. If lust is our sin, we will be forever unsatiated. If sloth is our sin, we will never know much as the internal turmoil that we create by our own lack of control.

🌸 "The sins of others are before our eyes; our own are behind our backs," the Roman poet Seneca wrote. The terrible truth has been spoken. We hide from others and from ourselves those things about ourselves, which, if we knew them, could save us. If we admitted our arrogance, faced our dishonesties, named our weaknesses—at least to ourselves—we would be consumed with kindness. We would know what God knows: that there is no one who is not struggling with the same kinds of things we are. There is no one who does not need and deserve our care.

🌸 "The most massive characters," E.H. Chapin wrote, "are seared with scars." It's what we endure, not what we avoid, that toughens us.

Counselors know that those who swallow a stone become a stone. There are pains so deeply hidden, even from ourselves that it is almost impossible to tell where they're coming from. When I find myself becoming what others avoid and what I myself do not want to be, it is time to reach into my heart and find the thorn that lives there.

The fourteenth-century English mystic, Julian of Norwich, taught that sin "is behoovable but that all shall be well." Sin is good for us, in other words, if we learn something about ourselves that leads us to become more mature than we were before it happened. It's called "learning the hard way" but it can, if we let it, be learning, nevertheless.

In Jesus' time, sickness was thought to be God's punishment for sin. When Jesus, in defiance of public opinion, gives sight to the blind man rather than leave him to what was seen as God's eternal punishment, it was a call to everybody to see sin differently. We are all called at some time in life to do the same.

When they listed all those sins they taught us, they forgot to list "prudence." What a pity. "A life spent making mistakes is not only more honorable," George Bernard Shaw wrote, "but more useful than a life spent in doing nothing."

Human failure is a very human thing. It is common to us all. What is not common is that we allow it to rule us. "What do you do in a monastery?" a disciple asked the old monastic. And the monastic answered simply, "We fall and we get up and we fall and we get up and we fall and we get up again." It is the "getting up" that requires help.

When we begin to own our errors, when we begin to take responsibility for our mistakes, we will have become adult. Then, we become spiritually mature.

Punishment is not the beginning of holiness, neither mine nor the person I'm punishing. It is, at best, what tests in me the struggle between correction and vengeance. "See everything; overlook a great deal; correct a little," Pope John XXIII wrote. Not a bad idea.

🐝 Sin is the sign that something is missing in our lives. "All sins are attempts to fill voids," Simone Weil wrote. Admonishment will only work, then, when we know what we're really looking for—and pursue it instead.

🐝 To make a sin undesirable is far more important than simply punishing people for doing it. The United States has five percent of the population of the world and twenty-five percent of its prisoners. Clearly our prison systems don't work. Isn't it time to ask ourselves why?

🐝 Anthony of Egypt, one of the great monastics of the desert wrote, "Do not trust in your own righteousness; do not grieve about a sin that is past and gone; and keep your tongue and your belly under control." Consider yourself admonished—and listen carefully.

🌿 Only when we lose hope in the mercy of God and in our own genuine determination to do better have we really abandoned ourselves to living a life beneath God's will for us. "It is more serious," John of Carpathos wrote, "to lose hope than to sin."

🌿 Failing to try to be more than our lowest self is a greater sin than the sin itself.

🌿 It is possible to break a person. It's rebuilding them that takes care, skill and commitment. "The idea that people sin and that therefore their behavior at times needs to be restricted, is fair enough; but the emphasis on control through fear, shame, and punitiveness," Anne Borrowdale writes, "does not create a society at ease with itself."

🌿 Before you punish the sin or humiliate the sinner, think carefully about what it was that saved you from your sins. "There is no saint without a past," the Persian proverb teaches. "And there is no sinner without a future."

❧ Be sure that when you preach against the sin, you do not sin yourself by attacking, exposing, and incriminating the sinner.

❧ It can take a long time to become the person we really want to be. As Mary Pickford writes, "You may have a fresh start any moment you choose, for this thing we call 'failure' is not the falling down, it is the staying down."

CHAPTER 3

Guilt and Conscience

"You can't absolve the Irish," the old joke goes: "They feel guilty for everything and sorry for nothing." It took me years to understand the implications of the remark but I finally got the point. Confession, penance, atonement all have to do with wrongdoing not with wrong thinking. There's a message there for all of us, perhaps. There's a difference between good guilt and bad guilt, between real guilt and false guilt. To grow as human beings, we need to be able to tell one from the other.

Guilt has gone out of fashion in the Western world. That's a shame. So much good comes out of guilt. Without it, what would ever drive us to change our lives for the better when we find ourselves losing our grip on conscience and conviction. We so often focus more on either denial or punishment than we do on the vision and the wisdom that can come out of recognizing our weaknesses and rededicating our lives to the values we hold and the ideals we seek.

This society is much more inclined, it seems, to talk about personal "growth" than it does about personal "guilt," more about strategies for self-promotion than about the development of inner vision. And the imbalance shows, both in the moral chaos that marks our social system and in the lack of moral limits that result from our almost fanatical pursuit of self-development in a highly individualistic culture. It's not difficult to understand what spawned the situation, of course. Disdainful of one extreme we have developed another and lost some of the most important spiritual wisdom in the lexicon of the human race as a result.

A highly religious culture with roots in Jansenism and Puritanism, we experienced the fear and self-loathing that comes out of hell-and-damnation sermons, darkly inflated concentration on human sinfulness, and the loss of a sense of natural human goodness. To combat such negative and exaggerated disdain of the human condition we created an environment that confuses the moral, the immoral, and the amoral. Now few people feel guilty about anything. It may be time to rediscover the glory of guilt and the mental and spiritual health that can come from it. Or is the notion of human responsibility a myth?

On Guilt

The first sign of healthy guilt is that we never feel guilty for the wrong things. Guilt always has something to do with failing to recognize my creature-hood or hurting someone else. Think of the Ten Commandments, the first three have to do with recognizing that God is God and not making ourselves the center of the universe; the next seven have to do with doing harm to others. As in, "Love God; love the other." Nothing else counts. Not really. The question that measures guilt is always, who was harmed?

The second sign of healthy guilt is that it is not exaggerated. Spiritual vision is the ability to see things as they are. Some of our struggles are serious; some of them are not. Some of our moral arm-wrestling matches of life are long-standing and need to be uprooted; some of them are only momentary breakdowns in an otherwise well-ordered soul.

The third sign of healthy guilt is that we do something about it and put the situation behind us. The purpose of guilt always is simply to enable us to recognize where we are failing the coming of the reign of God so that we can do better the next time. Its purpose is not to leave us wallowing in the past.

The things that bother my conscience are telling me something about the difference between what I am and what I want to be. It pays to listen to the small voice deep within. As Barbara Mraz says, "Guilt is an emotion that has periodically served me well."

Once I have felt guilt, I become a softer part of the human race. I am, then, prepared to be far more kind to other people who have also failed their own best aspirations than I could ever be to them without it.

Shame is the caution light of the heart. It stops us from giving ourselves over to what we do not want to become but now realize we are more capable of being.

"Oh, happy fault," the church sings in the Easter liturgy. Without the crucifixion, in other words, no resurrection. The message is painfully clear. Sometimes, with great sin, we get no great insights either.

Healthy guilt is neither scrupulosity nor rationalization. It does not make something out of nothing nor does it make nothing out of something. It simply looks personal failure in the eye and says, "I can do better than that."

The nice thing about guilt is that it proves that we are still alive. If we can still feel moral angst, we can feel everything else in life, too. Exaggerated guilt is called neurosis. On the other hand, exaggerated guiltlessness is neurotic, too. Both of those positions are out of touch with reality.

Never to feel guilty for anything I've done is to be spiritually immature. Always to feel guilty for things without substance is to be a spiritual invalid. Life is not about its end point. It is about the journey, about the way we're getting where we're going. Those moments of realization, which we call guilt, can change the course of that life for the better.

"Guilt is the one burden," Anais Nin writes, "that human beings cannot bear alone." Talking to someone else when we have disappointed ourselves is the key to being able to get a perspective on the events. What we do in the throes of emotional pressure measures only the moment, not the essential quality of character. Growth is just that: It is a process.

Guilt is not a matter of failing to meet the standards set by others. It involves the failures we suffer in keeping the standards we set for ourselves. If this society lacks guilt, it may be more that we lack values than we lack conscience. The problem is not that we're bad people. The problem is that we no longer agree on what to be good about.

God does not want us to be trapped by guilt. God wants us to be freed by it to make new judgments, to evaluate our lives, to rise another step on the ladder of the self.

Healthy guilt is not simply the fear of getting caught. That's just "fear of getting caught." Healthy guilt is knowing that there is something in us that is crying out to be ameliorated.

We must begin to see what we are, who we are, what we have. That's the beginning of real spiritual insight. How we get all these things, how we use them and develop the conscience to feel guilty about abusing any of them is the baseline of moral evaluation.

Real guilt is a process. Or as the wag wrote: King Solomon and King David led very many lives with very many concubines and very many wives until old age came creeping with very many qualms. Then Solomon wrote the proverbs and David wrote the psalms. Don't give up. Guilt, the grace of regret is often what comes long after the action is long done.

When we follow the life of Jesus, the laws he broke and why, we begin to see what is really important. That's what saves us from a kind of guilt that is either sick or superficial. Then we become concerned about the really big things of life: the outcasts of society, the poor, the children, the handicapped, the women, and the good of the other. If we ever developed a sense of guilt about those things, we would have a completely different world.

On Conscience

Conscience is the voice that reminds us that we have not lived up to our own best ideals. The psychologist Carl Jung wrote, "Deep down below the surface of the average conscience a still, small voice says to us, 'Something is out of tune.'"

The formation of conscience—the ability to recognize right and wrong, good and bad, truth and untruth, beauty and ugliness—is the major task of the human society. "Courage without conscience," Robert G. Ingersoll writes, "is a wild beast."

How can we ever become a fully human society if we never train ourselves to hear the voice of God, called conscience, within us?

Good development requires that we have good friends, friends who themselves listen for the voice of God in life. Or, as Abraham Lincoln put it, "Stand with anybody that stands right. Stand with them while they are right and part with them when they go wrong."

Conscience is what stops us just before we sin. Learning to listen to the voice deep within is the difference between living an average life and living a great life. Learning to choose good from good and best from better is the highest achievement of the human spirit.

"Every great mistake," Pearl Buck wrote, "has a halfway moment, a split second when it can be recalled and perhaps remedied."

CHAPTER 4

Forgive from Your Heart

The question is: What should we forgive and how do we do it?

An ancient monastic story gives a flash of an answer, so subtle, so swift that its meaning is easy to miss. A young woman, the story goes, is heavy with child and terrified of being executed for dishonoring the family name, accuses a revered old monk, who prayed daily at the city gates, of assaulting her and fathering the child. The people confronted the old man with the accusation. But the old man's only response to the frenzy of the crowd was a laconic,

"Is that so?" As he gazed into space and went on fingering his beads, the townspeople became even more infuriated and drove the culprit out of town.

Years later, the woman, exhausted by her guilt and wanting to relieve her burden and make restitution, finally admitted that it was her young lover, not the old monk, who fathered the child. In fear for his life as well as her own, she had lied about the attack. Stricken with compunction, the townspeople rushed to the hermitage in the hills where the old man was still saying his prayers and leading his simple life. "The girl has admitted that you did not assault her," the people shouted. "What are you going to do about that?" But all the old monk answered was, "Is that so?" and went right on fingering his beads.

It's a disturbing story for those who want justice. It's an even more disturbing story for those who feel that they have not been given it. But I have come to believe the story has a great deal to tell us about forgiveness: What other people do to us may have little or nothing to do with forgiveness. The fact is that there is nothing to forgive in life if and when we manage to create an interior life that has more to do with what we are than with what other people do to us. What we are inside ourselves determines how we react to others—no matter what they do. What we cannot forgive is what we have not supplied for ourselves independent of the responses of those around us. We've all heard people say, "You can't hurt me." Often, we've even said it ourselves. The problem is that few of us mean it.

🌸 It's one thing to "forgive" for the sake of civility. It is another thing to forgive "from the heart." Civility urges us to maintain the connections we have for the sake of our own advantage. The heart urges us to go beyond the hurt to the place where freedom lies and learning happens and trust is possible again, even if not here, not this.

Forgiveness frees me from the burden of anger. What I refuse to forgive continues to harm me. It consumes my heart, poisons my mind, drains my energies, and cements my soul. The anger, the hurt, the bitterness we carry from the past does little or nothing to harm the one who harmed us. It harms only us. It is acid poured on our own souls, eating away at the peace in us.

Once we know ourselves it is easy to forgive other people. The truth is that I am capable of everything they've ever done: Either I've never had the opportunity to do it or I've never been caught yet.

Forgiveness does not flow from the awareness that no matter how hurt I have been by someone I am far more than what they have taken away from me. That is not forgiveness at all. This kind of cheap forgiveness—forgiveness that is rushed in order to make everyone else feel good—is a sad show that never ends, always returns to haunt us, and can only pretend at freedom. It is, therefore, at best, also useless.

Forgiveness occurs when we don't need to hold a grudge anymore. It is when we are strong enough to be independent of whatever, whomever it was that so ruthlessly uncovered the need in us. Forgiveness is not the problem. It is living until the forgiveness comes that taxes all the strength we have.

Forgiveness is the gift that says two things: First, I am just as weak as everyone else in the human race and I know it. And, second, my inner life is too rich to be destroyed by anything outside of it.

Forgiveness and reconciliation is not the same thing. One enables us to move beyond the past. The other restores a relationship. The relationship is seldom as important as the restoration of inner peace that comes with recognizing that the past is past.

The inability to forgive another almost certainly arises out of an inability to forgive ourselves. When we refuse to give ourselves permission to be anything but perfect—as if failure did not bring its own lessons in life—we certainly are not able to forgive anyone else.

Some people think that forgiveness is incomplete until things are just as they were before. But the truth is that after great hurt, things are never what they were before; they can only be better or be nothing at all. Both of which are acceptable states of life. Forgiveness is what we need when we think we don't and what we give when we think we shouldn't.

We know we have forgiven someone when we can meet them with genuine acceptance in our hearts, wiser and warier than ever before, not of them but of our own past expectations of the relationship.

"Our greatest glory," Confucius wrote, "is not in never falling but in rising every time we fall." War against the war within the self by making peace with it early. Yes, we have been hurt; no, we will never trust the same situation again. But indeed we will be happy always because we know more about life now than we did before and, when we are totally involved in something else, we are more than capable of dealing with it.

We say, "forgive and forget" but I think the saying is upside down. The real truth may well be that until we have forgotten why we were angry we haven't really forgiven the wrong. But the only way to do that is to get intensely involved in something else.

If forgiveness has something to do with forgetting, pray that God is an amnesiac. It seems impossible to hope from God what we withhold ourselves.

If the message we're supposed to be getting is really, "Forgive us…as we forgive" it's time to let everything to the mercy of God, to put down unholy righteousness, to purge ourselves of grudges, and to move where we're welcome, uncaring and where we're not.

The Spanish proverb reads, "If I die, I forgive you; if I recover, we shall see." Why are you laughing?

To forgive someone is not to say that what they did to you is all right. It simply says that what they did to you, cannot, in the end, destroy you.

Hannah Arendt wrote: "Forgiveness is the key to action and freedom." Why stay back where it hurts? Why stay stuck in the swamp of bitterness? Let the end to God and go where life has new promise. That's where God is calling you so why stay where the voice has gone silent?

🌸 "Without forgiveness," Roberto Assagioli wrote, "life is governed by an endless cycle of resentment and retaliation." What a waste of time. What a loss of perspective. What a diminishment of vision. What a poor investment of a life.

🌸 When we cry after a quarrel, the source of those tears reveals the real nature of the argument, the real hope for reconciliation. To cry because we have hurt another reveals one thing; to cry because we feel the pinch of our own humiliation and psychological battering in the struggle unmasks another agenda entirely. Learning to tell the difference between the two makes the difference between a life lived in truth and a life lived in shadow.

🌸 The only persons worthy to be someone else's confessor are people who know their own weaknesses—and their own efforts to wrestle them to the floor of their hearts. Those people are kind.

🌸 It takes no strength at all to require restitution. What takes strength is to be full enough of other things to be able to forego it.

🌸 "Life is an adventure in forgiveness," Norman Cousins said. You will, in other words, have lots of opportunity to practice. Don't wait too long to start or life will have gone by before you ever lived it.

🌸 To withhold forgiveness is the adoration of the past when it is the present that demands the best of us.

🌸 Beware of premature forgiveness: the kind that absolves another person without taking the time or making the effort to examine what the bitterness is saying to our own souls about our own needs and expectations.

Forgiveness does not ignore responsibility; actions have consequences. But forgiveness does not tolerate vengeance. To jail criminals for life in order to protect the public is one thing; to become killers in order to punish them is vengeance. Where does that fit in a Divine schema that says, "Vengeance is mine; I will repay," says God.

A preacher stood over the bed of a dying man shouting, "Renounce Satan; renounce Satan and be forgiven!" The dying man opened one eye, looked at the preacher and said, "Sure, easy for you to say, Pastor, but in my situation I don't dare alienate anybody." The old man may have a point: You have to wonder if forgiveness that comes with strings attached is really forgiveness at all.

❧ The failure to forgive, the unyielding memory of the debt, is too great a burden to carry. It smothers the joy out of life. It blocks our own ability to move. It makes growth impossible. It traps us in the juices of the snake that bit us. That is not the mercy of the forgiving God who wipes out the past and everyday, makes all things new again. To forego the need for requital releases us as well as our debtor from further harm. We free the debtor from shame and ourselves from bitterness.

❧ It is only when we forgive that peace comes. When we suppress the pain that comes from sin, when we seek retribution rather than a new beginning, then the evil of vengeance and the failure of forgetfulness reproduce evil in abundance.

❧ The poet Jose Marti wrote, "When others are weeping blood, what right have I to weep tears?" Real justice requires that we commiserate with those who suffer so that we can find the reason within us to put an end to the oppression.

❧ Sir William Blackstone, legendary English barrister, wrote, "It is better that ten guilty persons escape than that one innocent suffer." But if we believed that, we would not be one of the countries in the world that practices capital punishment in the name of justice. Some hallmark for a nation that calls itself Christian.

❧ Thomas à Kempis, considered one of the more rigorous of the world's spiritual directors, wrote, "Be assured that if you knew all, you would pardon all." There are circumstances behind every circumstance. Circumstances may not always justify what a person does but they always explain it, make it understandable. We may not know them but they are always there. Believe that and you will never be closed off to anybody in the world.

❧ Forgiveness frees me from the burden of anger. What I refuse to forgive continues to harm me. It consumes my heart, poisons my mind, drains my energies and cements my soul.

❧ There are some pains that can never be healed because those who inflicted them have no desire to heal them. In that case, the only recourse is to build for yourself a new life around the hurt rather than allow the hurt to smother the rest of life.

❧

The Creed is talking about forgiveness for sin, real sin, not merely the invalidation of some kind of gross but basically benign misunderstanding. Harm has been done. Trust has been betrayed. Goodness has been foresworn for personal advantage. Someone has, like Cain, ceased to be my keeper and slain my heart. Then forgiveness, not dissembling, is imperative. This violation of ourselves is not about social formality. This is about relationships rent. This is about repair. This is about the need for real forgiveness, not cheap forgiveness, the kind counseled for the sake of a false peace. "Oh, don't let it bother you" is not an answer to sin. "Just don't pay any attention to it" does not erase the pain in the heart. "Just forget it. Put it down" dismisses both the sinner and the sinned-against. It asks for tawdry, cocktail-party forgiveness, for "niceness" that fails to diminish the pain, that leaves the sore raw but covered over by the cosmetics of civility waiting to erupt again. This is not the kind of forgiveness that makes for peace, either between people or between nations.

Real forgiveness relies, like the forgiveness of God, on full acknowledgment of the act that impaled the heart of a person, full knowledge of the motive, full acceptance of the human condition: People do these things. It is not so much what a person does to us that is the essence of forgiveness. It is what we do because of the sorrow we suffer that counts.

Premature forgiveness doesn't work. All it does is to substitute formality where genuine connection should be. It leaves the process of forgiveness incomplete. It risks the possibility of submerging feelings that will only rise again in us, displaced perhaps but there nevertheless, until we embrace them, face them, and, perhaps still smarting from the blow of them, move on beyond what cannot be changed to another point in life. Then, all the ruptures can be repaired and forgiveness can be total because the fruits of sin have finally come to full. Not because they were good but because we went beyond them.

That is divine forgiveness, the awareness that though evil has been done, the spirit is whole. (Joan Chittister, *In Search of Belief*)

CHAPTER 5

Healing and Forgiveness

"There is a time to weep…and a time to heal," the Book of Ecclesiastes teaches.

The relationship between healing and pain, pain and healing is an ancient one. But I have asked myself repeatedly whether or not it is really possible to heal the ruptures of life. And, even if it is, why bother when it seems that when one thing is healed we then find new ways to hurt, new things to weep over?

To talk about the spirituality of healing and its place and process in our own lives, means I must deal with questions like these:

- Do tears hurt or help us?

- What is the relationship between my pain and the pain around me

- What happens when we stop weeping?

- What does healing do for the healer?

- How does healing happen?

With those questions in mind, I want simply to share some of the insights of the ages about the links between healing and weeping that have kept me going despite the often discouraging awareness of this ever repeating cycle—and which convince me that it is possible to bear the despair pain brings and endure the struggle healing requires and emerge even more vibrantly human after it than we were before.

Or, to put it another way, I want to explore the value and the place of weeping in life.

The Gift of Tears

In fact, one of the most ancient of monastic devotions is the prayer for the gift of tears, the grace to recognize and unmask the tragedy of evil around us as well as the indifference within us that enables us to ignore it, to take it for granted, to accept it.

Evagrius of Ponticus, one of the early desert monastics (349-399), in fact, counseled young monastics: "First pray for the gift of tears, to soften by compunction the inherent hardness of your soul."

And fifteen centuries later, George Eliot wrote, too, "The beginning of compunction is the beginning of new life."

The point is clear: Weeping is a very life-giving thing. It wizens the soul of the individual and it sounds alarms in society. The Book of Ecclesiastes may be nowhere more correct than here. There is definitely a time for weeping. If we do not weep on the personal level, we shall never understand other human beings.

If we do not weep on the public level at the inhuman conditions that trap those around us: for the part-time employed, for instance who have no cars to get them to the jobs they need; for the innocent in the Middle East who sit in bunkers and basements waiting for the next bombs to fall; for the women of the world who are trapped in unholy religious silence and told it's God's will; if we do not weep for these and those like them; if we remain dry-eyed and indifferent—we are less than human ourselves.

There are, in other words, some things that simply ought not to be endured. We must always cope with evil, yes, but we must never, ever adjust to it either ours or anyone else's.

There are things we should all be weeping about. What we weep for, you see, measures what we are and determines what we do, as well.

Weeping signals that it is time to change things in life. John Tillotson wrote once: "Though all afflictions are evils in themselves, yet they are good for us, because they discover to us our disease and tend to our cure."

Without our tears, we have no hope of healing because we do not begin to admit the anguish. Indeed, ironically, of all the expressions of human emotion in the lexicon of life, weeping may be the most life-giving.

The point is that our tears expose us. They lay us bare both to others and to ourselves. You see, what we cry about is what we care about. So the question underlying our concentration on healing is: What have you wept about lately? What brings tears to your eyes? What is it that you cannot hear about without shedding the tears of the soul?

The truth is that until we cry about what sears our souls, strains our hopes and dreams and ideals— stand them toe to toe, wrestle them to the ground of our souls, staunch the blood of it—we will never get beyond the wounds.

In fact, the very process of human development demands—merits even—a tear or two. We cry at death and we cry at birth. We cry at endings and we cry at beginnings, too. How else can we move from place to place, phase to phase of life, and mark the passages as we go unless we allow ourselves to feel, to appreciate either the meaning the past has had on our lives or the effort the present demands?

But there is a public dimension to tears as well as a personal one. The ancients talked, too, about the "gift of tears," as the grace of sorrow for sin. To have the "gift of tears" is to have the heart to care about what we do to others—to have the conscience to care about what we have done to destroy creation—to have the commitment to self to care about what we have done to our own bodies or minds in the name of personal "freedom."

Indeed, tears attune us to ourselves and tears attune us to the rest of the human race, as well. Once we have suffered, the suffering of others falls upon our softened hearts and we become more human members of the human race. We possess a spirituality of weeping that is electrifying in its aliveness of heart.

No, never underestimate the spiritual power of tears.

The Rabbis tell us that a man who was afflicted with a terrible disease complained to Rabbi Israel that his suffering interfered with his learning and his praying. And the Rabbi put his hand on the man's shoulder and said: "Tell me, friend, how do you know that studying is really more pleasing to God than what you will learn about life through suffering?"

No doubt about it: It's not possible to talk about healing until we talk about weeping. Healing depends on what we have learned to weep about.

The Healing That Comes out of Tears

That's why, I'm convinced, the Book of Ecclesiastes deals with both topics. But it is very deceptive. Ecclesiastes reads with such simplicity: There is "a time to weep, a time to heal" it insists—sounding monotonous and droning, hypnotic and obvious.

But if we struggle with the themes in it, we also begin to realize that what is actually being said by statements like: "There is a time to weep… a time to heal" is not one message, it's two. On the one hand, it is saying, that there's a period of time in every human life when the process of being healed, of coming beyond my own woundedness, may itself be life's greatest project.

But on the other hand, it is equally clear, that there is not only a time in every life for a person to care about the sufferings of other people—to weep for them—but that there is also some obligation to do something to alleviate them, to heal them.

Isn't the implication, then, that healing, the cauterization of wounds, is part of the essential rhythm of life on both the personal and the public level? That we all need it? That each of us needs it?

Mustn't we all go through suffering someday or run the risk, ironically, of never being whole because we have never known what it is to be wounded. As a result, we never become able to repent the woundedness of others and raise them up to live again for all our sakes. Suffering, after all, is surely not for its own sake only. The Christian scriptures, for instance, are quite direct about it.

In the Parable of the Good Samaritan, Jesus tells of a traveler who, having been mugged by robbers, was left stripped, beaten, and bleeding on a public road. First, a Levite, an official of the temple, and then a priest, the agent of temple sacrifice—holy men both we are led to think—pass by the broken one. The Scripture says they pass "on the other side." They go as far away from the violence, the need, the pain as possible.

Then a Samaritan—the national and religious outcast of that Jewish society—comes by. And the healing begins. The Samaritan, having suffered himself, recognizes the suffering of the other. He understands pain and rejection. He knows how misery feels. He knows what a sense of abandonment can do for a person. So, he reaches out beyond himself.

The Samaritan pours oil, costly medicines for those times, on the beaten one's wounds. He carried him to an inn on the "back of his own beast." He pays for his care. He simply ignores the assumptions and the prejudices of the society around him and then the healing begins.

Healing does not begin with the moralizing of the righteous who avoided the unclean one—as this society, for instance, avoids AIDS or alcoholics, welfare mothers or gay neighbors. Healing does not begin with the piosity of the pious who say that such things are not what religion is all about.

No, healing only begins when the one who understood suffering, who had wept himself, then wept over the suffering of another. The story of the Samaritan makes obvious for us the fundamental elements of the healing process—the ones beyond technique or politics, civic charity or public niceties.

First, the Samaritan simply faces the pain. He admits it. He honors it. The Samaritan does not ignore suffering or recoil from it or try to minimize it or explain it away. He knows calamity when he sees it—anywhere and in anyone. Without the Good Samaritans in life who enable us all to face our woundedness, to attend to the wounds in ourselves, we have no capacity for the pain of others. And healing is not possible.

Second, the Samaritan shows us, too, that healing requires us to risk old attitudes, to explore new values and even to change some of our petrified beliefs. The model of the Samaritan is very clear: Healing depends on our own resolve to transcend our canonical confines, to go out of our way to be, to think, to do what we would not, under any standard circumstances, choose to do otherwise.

Third, the Samaritan shows us that when I heal the other, I heal something in myself as well. The Parable of the Good Samaritan, you see, is not about the curing of one person, a wounded stranger. No, this story is about the healing of two people—the stranger and the Samaritan—both of whom carry the scars of abuse as do all of us at all times.

In this case one has been beaten in body, the

other in soul. One has been wounded by the physical brutality of people around him; the other has been wounded by ideas that cripple and limit and bind a person to small, small worlds.

But the Samaritan and the stranger are not the only ones in the story who bear wounds. The priest and the Levite are maimed too—whether they know it or not. The priest, the professional religious, has been taught to ignore the wounds of those who do not meet with religious approval and thinks himself virtuous for ignoring them. His wound is a spiritual one.

The Levite, the relentless custodian of temple rituals and a pillar of his community, simply forgives himself the obligation to be a full human being and so hurries on too busy to stop, too narcissistic to care. Being "religious" is enough for him. His wound is a communal one.

One posture teaches us fear and loathing. The other perspective teaches us the kind of indifference and insensitivity that can come with idol worship.

Whatever the situation, the end result is pain. Those who fail to transcend their own inner boundaries in order to heal the wounded, go on living in their own wounds forever.

Finally, the Good Samaritan has something to say to us about the very process of healing. Who has not known what it is to be hurt by either hate or neglect, to be passed by on the road of life by those from whom we thought we could certainly expect help?

Who has not known what it is to be targeted for scorn or rejection or jealousy or misinterpretation or stereotyping? Who has not felt the stultifying effects of ideas that make us captive to the agendas and ambitions of others and leave us as much oppressed as oppressor? What is the process, then, of coming to wholeness again, once the bonds of human community have been broken? What repairs the breaking of a golden cord?

The Healing Process and Our Part in It

The Samaritan, the priest, and the Levite, models of the healing process and our part in it, give us clear warning that we cannot heal ourselves of our wounds by clinging to them.

To be healed we need to want to be healed. We cannot wear injustice like a red badge of courage and simply hope to rise from it. We must move beyond it, outside of it, despite it ourselves.

Healing depends on our wanting to be well, to be larger than our pain, stronger than our woundedness.

"Will you cure the people who come to you?" the disciple asked the Holy One.

"Oh, people don't come to be cured," the Holy One answered. "They come for relief. A cure would require change and that's the last thing in the world they want to do."

I must choose not to imprison myself in my own pain, in the creeds and jingoisms, in the biases and prejudices that cut me off from the pain of the rest of the world. There is more to life than that.

Healing, the Samaritan shows us, requires that we set out to find whatever new life we can find to tide us through the terror of the abandonment, the degradation of the abuse. It is time to get a life instead of to mourn one.

When the beating is over, there is nothing to do but to get up and go on, in a different direction to be sure, but on, definitely on. We must put our hope in risk and find it challenging, in self and find it strong, in newness and find it enough.

Healing is a process of refusing to be wounded unto death of beginning to be bigger of mind and soul than we ever thought we could be.

Healing, we see in both the Samaritan and the stranger, requires us to trust the process of growing. Healing comes for both the beaten and the intellectually bound when they step across the lines in their minds and hope that this time—in this person, in this situation—they will find the acceptance and the understanding, the care and the security they need to join the human community one more time.

I will know that healing has come when I have been able to desensitize myself to the indignity of the hurt by telling it to death until I bore even myself with the story.

Finally, I need to become a Samaritan myself. The whole world needs Samaritans, healers, who understand pain themselves and who are therefore most qualified to take the wounded into the arms of their hearts, listen to the pain of the other, enable them to talk, allow them to cry.

Samaritans transcend their own small lives and learn about the human condition, something they could never have come to without having become healers themselves. The whole world—its poor and lonely; its displaced and angry; its deprived and robbed of the resources of life—needs Samaritans who listen and understand, tend to their wounds, and get them help. At that point, we rise from our graves of pain—persons and peoples alike—a new creation, a sign of hope to generations to come.

So, in the end, in the face of the pain of the world

we have three choices. We can choose to become totally desensitized to the mayhem and the devastation it has left in its way. Or we can simply turn away from it, aware of it but unwilling to engage with it anymore. But there is a third choice, more true to the spiritual tradition that shaped our culture, that bred our souls, a choice more cleansing of our psyches, and, in the long run, more effective. We can, with the second century monastics of the desert, rediscover the power of "the gift of tears."

We can allow ourselves to recognize and unmask the tragedy of evil in the society around us. We can refuse the sense of powerlessness within us that enables us to ignore it, to take it for granted, to accept it. We can, as the spiritual people we claim to be, begin to regret, to repent, to decry, to grieve the evil around us—and to insist that it be changed!

Remorse is not nothing. Grief is not useless. It changes the heart of a people. It cautions them to think better, to think and speak and work in new ways, before they are once again tempted to bomb and beat a people into submission, into "freedom." It makes them new—and, eventually, the whole society with them. Then, one person at a time, the world finally learns to feel. It's called a "soul."

It is possible that we are now approaching the margins of the human condition. We are drowning in insensitivity. We are escaping into escape. We have lost the capacity to weep ourselves into the fullness of our humanity.

It seems to me that until we are willing to face what is happening in our name in this world—to regret it, to own the agony of it—it will go on. And we will go on, numbly, totally unaware of the diminishing effects of this culture of violence on both those with whom we fail to weep and on ourselves.

Once upon a time, the people said to Thucydides, "Thucydides, when will justice come to Athens?" And he answered, "Justice will not come to Athens until those who are not oppressed are as indignant about it as those who are."

Clearly, weeping and healing are one and the same thing. Our only real questions then are: Over what do we ourselves weep? And, because of our tears: What are we reaching out to heal?

I urge you to listen to the Samaritans of our own time and to ask yourself where you yourselves fit in the great, the ultimate, the most humane human enterprise of the healing of the world. Only together can we possibly do the great works of healing, which in our time are waiting to be done by those "who cross the street," who do not "stay at a distance" from the pain of the world but whose hearts are great enough, human enough to weep for it.

For the sake of the world, for the sake of the planet—and if that is not good enough, for the sake of the children—I am begging you to weep and heal. Weep and heal. Weep and weep and weep so that finally, one day, we may all really be holy and all really be healed.

MORE SPIRITUAL READING

Songs of the Heart *Reflections on the Psalms*
JOAN CHITTISTER

Sr. Joan offers poignant, challenging reflections on 25 psalms, each offering a spiritual oasis away from the stresses of the world. In reflecting on these psalms, readers will find new meaning at the core of life and then make songs of their own.

136 pages, hardcover • **$12.95** • **order 958351** • **978-1-58595-835-1**

The Breath of the Soul *Reflections on Prayer*
JOAN CHITTISTER

These soul-searing reflections touch the heart and mind and challenge readers to see prayer as the way to touch God in all that they do. This is great spiritual reading for all who long for God to be at the core of their lives.

144 pages, hardcover • **$12.95** • **order 957477** • **978-1-58595-747-7**

Faith, Hope, and a Bird Called George *A Spiritual Fable*
MICHAEL MORWOOD

Through this simple spiritual fable, Michael Morwood offers an invitation to all believers to reflect, pray, discuss, and grow so that they too might experience God, Jesus, and the Spirit more deeply and profoundly.

152 pages, hardcover • **$12.95** • **order 958276** • **978-1-58595-827-6**

1-800-321-0411
www.23rdpublications.com

TWENTY THIRD *23rd*